Sweet and Simple
PARTY CAKES

MAY CLEE-CADMAN
of *Maisie Fantaisie*

D&C
David and Charles

A DAVID & CHARLES BOOK
Copyright © David & Charles Limited 2008

David & Charles is an F+W Publications Inc. company
4700 East Galbraith Road, Cincinnati, OH 45236

First published in the UK & US in 2008

Text and designs copyright © May Clee-Cadman 2008
Photography copyright © David & Charles 2008

A catalogue record for this book is available from the British Library.

ISBN-13: 978-0-7153-2694-7 hardback
ISBN-10: 0-7153-2694-5 hardback

ISBN-13: 978-0-7153-2687-9 paperback
ISBN-10: 0-7153-2687-2 paperback

Printed in China by SNP Leefung
for David & Charles
Brunel House   Newton Abbot   Devon

Commissioning Editor: Jennifer Fox-Proverbs
Desk Editor: Bethany Dymond
Art Editor: Sarah Underhill
Designer: Lisa Wyman
Project Editor: Juliet Bracken
Production Controller: Bev Richardson
Photographer: Ginette Chapman

Visit our website at www.davidandcharles.co.uk

David & Charles books are available from all good bookshops;
alternatively you can contact our Orderline on 0870 9908222
or write to us at FREEPOST EX2 110, D&C Direct, Newton Abbot,
TQ12 4ZZ (no stamp required UK only); US customers call 800-289-0963
and Canadian customers call 800-840-5220.

Contents

Pastels

Whites

Brights

Introduction

What gives me the most pleasure after finishing a cake? Simple, watching people's faces light up when they see it. My hope with this book is for you to experience the joy and satisfaction of creating a delicious masterpiece for yourself.

I've been making cakes since I was a little girl. My mother, sister and I would spend long, blissful afternoons in the kitchen, trying out new recipes from one of our many cake and pudding books. Years on and the smell of vanilla and fruitcake still hangs in the air, and I feel so fortunate to be dreamily reliving my childhood in my chosen career.

Here, I have picked a selection of my all-time favourite cakes and given simple, step-by-step instructions so you can recreate them and amaze yourself. Cakes that are simple to make but staggering to behold, such as Butterfly Kisses (page 42), Wedding Sunflowers (page 100) and the Birthday Parcel cake (page 92); all of which are guaranteed to create an absolute sensation at any event.

If you are short for time, discover the many ways of adapting the designs to create sensational cupcakes and mini cakes. The smaller versions look just as fabulous as the larger cakes and will suit every occasion, whether it's a formal or informal affair. You can even create your own gorgeous wedding cake entirely from mini cakes, as I have done in the pretty Lavender and Hearts design on page 60.

Each cake is beautifully photographed so you can see every detail that makes it special, and there are clear step-by-step instructions explaining how it's done. Feel free to adapt the designs to suit your occasion, whether it's changing the template, colour, shape or sizes; use the book as a tool rather than a rulebook.

I consider the taste of the cake to be just as important as the decoration, so I have also included a selection of cake recipes on pages 14–17 for you to get started with. Baking cakes is good for the heart and soul so give yourself the time to enjoy it. I guarantee your cakes will come out of the oven fluffier because you've baked with a smile on your face!

Lastly, don't wait for an occasion to make a cake, make an occasion around your cake! Most of all, enjoy the whole process – the making is just as enjoyable as the eating! So why not take some time, clear some space, get out your mixing bowl and turn on the oven!

May Clee-Cadman

How to Use this Book

Over the next few pages you will find the guide to the cake making techniques you need to create the designs in the book. This covers:

Cake making equipment – both essentials and more specialist items you may not need every time

Four delicious traditional cake recipes

Different types of icing and fillings, and how to work with them

Putting a cake together – icing the board, levelling a cake and assembling tiers with dowels

How to make cupcakes and mini cakes

If you are new to cake making, I suggest you read through this section of the book carefully before starting on your first cake, so you get to know the techniques involved and feel confident about using them. You should find them easy to understand from the step-by-step instructions and photographs. I also explain how to create the decorations for each design using a combination of sugarpaste, flowerpaste and royal icing, along with details of any flowers or other embellishments I am using.

If you are a more experienced cake maker, you will probably enjoy adapting the designs to suit a particular occasion or theme. I am providing further inspiration showing how you can do this by changing the colour, shape or size of your cake or decorations.

Techniques

Equipment

Here is the complete list of all the cake making equipment used for the designs in the book, but you will not need everything every time. Check the materials and equipment lists at the beginning of each chapter for the specific tools required.

1 **Greaseproof paper** To line the cake tins.

2 **Spirit level** To ensure that stacked cakes are level.

3 **Large and small palette knives** For smoothing buttercream and jam onto cakes.

4 **Pastry brush** For brushing water onto under iced cakes.

5 **Large rolling pin** For rolling out the sugarpaste cake coverings.

6 **Small rolling pin** For rolling out the flowerpaste and icing for the sugarcraft details.

7 **Icing smoother** For achieving a really smooth icing finish.

8 **Small plastic board** To roll out flowerpaste and icing for the sugarcraft details.

9 **Cocktail sticks** For use with the food colourings.

10 **Flower foam pad** Also called a celpad. Used to thin and curl the flowerpaste.

11 **Cake boards** Drum and thin hardboard, various sizes, round and square (see specific chapters for size required).

12 **Plastic dowels** Used to support tiered cakes.

13 **Paintbrushes** A range of sizes for painting, dusting and dabbing.

14 **PME1 bone tool** Used with the flower foam pad to form and curl flower petals.

15 **Cutters** PME sunflower cutter (70mm), small leaf cutter, butterfly cutter, large blossom plunger cutter, small blossom cutter, large daisy cutter, 19mm daisy cutter, holly plunger cutter, circle cutter, small star cutter.

16 **PME piping nozzles** No.1.5, No.2, No.3, No.43, No.4, No.ST50.

17 **Tilting turntable** For use when a cake is being decorated.

18 **Stay fresh plastic mat** Used to stop flowerpaste drying out.

19 **White stamens** For butterfly antenna.

20 **Various food colourings** To create the icing colours used in the designs.

21 **Edible lustre** Snowflake, brilliant gold, to make cakes and decorations sparkle and shimmer.

22 **Edible glitters** Used as a highlight on rose petals.

23 **PME6 Scriber needle** Used to score details onto cakes.

24 **Sharp knife or scalpel** For cutting straight edges or shapes precisely.

25 **Ruler** To help with levelling cakes.

26 **Small silver chain** Used to create a swag line.

27 **Florists tape and wire in green and white** For fresh flower details and to wire up sugar flower displays.

28 **Butterfly former card** For creating a butterfly shape.

Lining Tins and Preparation

To maximize your enjoyment of the whole cake making process, always start with a clear workspace, with all the equipment and ingredients you need to hand. You will also have some time in between each task (while your cakes cool, or your icing sets) to make flowers and to clean down your work place in preparation for the next task.

Lining tins

A greaseproof lining is the best way to prevent the cake sticking to the bottom and sides of the cake tin. This is cut precisely to fit the tin and attached with melted butter or sunflower oil.

Materials and equipment

Cake tin

Greaseproof paper

Pencil

Scissors

Melted butter or sunflower oil

Pastry brush

one Lay out a sheet of greaseproof paper and place your tin on top. Draw around it and cut out the circle or square (**a**).

two From the roll, cut a length of greaseproof paper 11cm (4½in) wide. Fold the length in half and in half again. Cut snips, approx 2.5cm (1in) deep, along the bottom of the paper, then unfold (**b**).

three Melt some butter (or use sunflower oil) and brush it over the inside base and round the sides of the tin (**c**).

four Stick the length of greaseproof paper around the sides of the tin allowing the tabs to sit on the base. Place the cut out circle or square on top, covering the tabs.

five If you are making a fruit cake, cover the outside of the tin with folded newspaper and tie on with string.

tip You can use spray sunflower oil instead of butter. This can be purchased from most well stocked supermarkets.

You can't beat the wonderful smell of fresh baking and the satisfaction you feel when your cake rises to perfection.

Cake Recipes and Charts

Here are the recipes for the cakes I like to make as the base for my designs. I've included charts so you can easily vary the quantities to make a larger or smaller version. And, of course, they're all perfect for cupcakes or mini cakes (see page 30).

Basic vanilla sponge cake

ROUND	15cm (6in)	18cm (7in)	20cm (8in)	22cm (9in)	25cm (10in)	28cm (11in)	30cm (12in)
SQUARE	12cm (5in)	15cm (6in)	18cm (7in)	20cm (8in)	22cm (9in)	25cm (10in)	28cm (11in)
Margarine/ softened butter	150g (5oz)	150g (5oz)	200g (7oz)	250g (9oz)	350g (12oz)	450g (1lb)	550g (1lb 4oz)
Caster sugar	150g (5oz)	150g (5oz)	200g (7oz)	250g (9oz)	350g (12oz)	450g (1lb)	550g (1lb 4oz)
Self-raising flour	150g (5oz)	150g (5oz)	200g (7oz)	250g (9oz)	350g (12oz)	450g (1lb)	550g (1lb 4oz)
Eggs	3	3	4	5	7	9	11
Vanilla extract	½ teaspoon	½ teaspoon	¾ teaspoon	1 teaspoon	1 teaspoon	1½ teaspoons	2 teaspoons
Baking time (approx)	50 mins	50 mins	50 mins	1 hr	1 hr 15 mins	1 hr 30 mins	1 hr 30 mins

Method

one Preheat the oven to 160ºC (315ºF/Gas Mark 2–3). Line the base of your tin only (see page 12) and grease the sides.

two Beat the margarine and sugar together until they are light and fluffy.

three Add the eggs one at a time, beating well after each addition.

four Sift in the flour and mix thoroughly.

five Add the vanilla extract.

six Pour the mixture into the tin, place in the oven and bake for the guide time listed in the recipe, or until the cake is lightly golden and a skewer inserted into the centre comes out clean.

seven Leave the cake to stand in the tin for five minutes before turning out onto a wire rack to cool.

Flavour variations

Quantities are for a 20cm (8in) round (4-egg) cake. You need to modify them for a different size cake.

Citrus – Add the zest of 1½–2 lemons or oranges to the mix (but NOT the juice).

Coffee – Add 50ml (2floz) espresso or concentrated instant coffee.

Banana – Add 1 very ripe mashed banana per egg.

Almond – Replace ¼ of the self-raising flour with an equal weight of ground almonds, two drops of almond extract and ½ teaspoon baking powder.

Carrot cake

ROUND	15cm (6in)	18cm (7in)	20cm (8in)	22cm (9in)	25cm (10in)	28cm (11in)	30cm (12in)
SQUARE	12cm (5in)	15cm (6in)	18cm (7in)	20cm (8in)	22cm (9in)	25cm (10in)	28cm (11in)
Plain flour	170g (6oz)	250g (9oz)	440g (1lb)	500g (1lb 2oz)	750g (1lb 11oz)	875g (1lb 15oz)	1kg (2lb 3oz)
Soft brown sugar	120g (4oz)	175g (6oz)	300g (10½oz)	350g (12oz)	525g (1lb 3oz)	610g (1lb 6oz)	700g (1lb 9oz)
Caster sugar	120g (4oz)	175g (6oz)	300g (10½oz)	350g (12oz)	525g (1lb 3oz)	610g (1lb 6oz)	700g (1lb 9oz)
Sunflower oil	120ml (4 floz)	165ml (5 floz)	300ml (10 floz)	350ml (12 floz)	500ml (18 floz)	610ml (20 floz)	700ml (24 floz)
Sour cream	40ml (1 floz)	50ml (1½ floz)	100ml (3 floz)	120ml (4 floz)	175ml (6 floz)	210ml (7 floz)	230ml (8 floz)
Vanilla	1 teaspoon	2 teaspoons	3 teaspoons	4 teaspoons	6 teaspoons	7 teaspoons	8 teaspoons
Desiccated coconut	25g (1oz)	75g (3oz)	130g (4oz)	150g (5oz)	225g (8oz)	275g (10oz)	300g (11oz)
Bicarbonate of soda	½ teaspoon	1 teaspoon	1½ teaspoons	2 teaspoons	3 teaspoons	3½ teaspoons	4 teaspoons
Cinnamon	¾ teaspoon	2 teaspoons	3 teaspoons	4 teaspoons	6 teaspoons	7 teaspoons	8 teaspoons
Mixed spice	½ teaspoon	1 teaspoon	1½ teaspoons	2 teaspoons	3 teaspoons	3½ teaspoons	4 teaspoons
Salt	¼ teaspoon	½ teaspoon	¾ teaspoon	1 teaspoon	1½ teaspoons	1¾ teaspoons	2 teaspoons
Grated carrot	200g (7oz)	300g (11oz)	525g (1lb 3oz)	600g (1lb 5oz)	900g (2lb)	1050g (2lb 4oz)	1200g (2lb 10oz)
Orange zest	2	2	3	3	4	5	5
Eggs	2	3	5	6	9	11	12
Sultanas (soaked in brandy if desired!)	100g (3½oz)	150g (6oz)	200g (7oz)	250g (9oz)	300g (10½oz)	350g (12oz)	400g (14oz)
Rum or brandy	25ml (1 floz)	35ml (1¼ floz)	55ml (2 floz)	65ml (2¼ floz)	75ml (2¾ floz)	90ml (3¼ floz)	100ml (3½ floz)
Baking time	1 hr 30 mins	1 hr 45 mins	2 hrs	2 hrs 15 mins	2 hrs 30 mins	2hrs 45 mins	3 hrs

Method

one Preheat the oven to 160°C (315°F/Gas Mark 2–3).

two Line the cake tin, sides and base (see page 12).

three Mix the sunflower oil, sour cream, vanilla, eggs and orange zest together. Then add the two types of sugar.

four In a separate bowl, sift the flour, spices, bicarbonate of soda and salt together.

five Combine the dry ingredients with the wet mixture.

six Add the grated carrot to the mixture along with the coconut and sultanas.

seven Bake for the guide time listed in the recipe or until a skewer inserted into the centre comes out clean.

tip You will need two vanilla sponge cakes of the same size to make a sandwich, whilst carrot cake and chocolate fudge cake are baked in one tin and cut in half.

Traditional fruit cake

ROUND	15cm (6in)	18cm (7in)	20cm (8in)	22cm (9in)	25cm (10in)	28cm (11in)	30cm (12in)
SQUARE	12cm (5in)	15cm (6in)	18cm (7in)	20cm (8in)	22cm (9in)	25cm (10in)	28cm (11in)
Mixed fruit (sultanas, currants, raisins)	495g (1lb 2oz)	800g (1lb 12oz)	1000g (2lb 3oz)	1250g (2lb 12oz)	2400g (5lb 5oz)	1925g (4lb 4oz)	2350g (5lb 3oz)
Glacé cherries	25g (1oz)	50g (2oz)	75g (2½oz)	110g (4oz)	150g (5oz)	200g (7oz)	225g (8oz)
Mixed peel	25g (1oz)	50g (2oz)	75g (2½oz)	110g (4oz)	150g (5oz)	200g (7oz)	225g (8oz)
Oranges (zest and juice)	1	2	2	3	3	3	4
Softened butter	175g (6oz)	225g (8oz)	275g (10oz)	400g (14oz)	500g (1lb 2oz)	600g (1lb 5oz)	825g (1lb 13oz)
Dark brown sugar	175g (6oz)	225g (8oz)	275g (10oz)	400g (14oz)	500g (1lb 2oz)	600g (1lb 5oz)	825g (1lb 13oz)
Eggs	2	3	5	6	9	11	13
Plain flour	175g (6oz)	225g (8oz)	275g (10oz)	400g (14oz)	500g (1lb 2oz)	600g (1lb 5oz)	825g (1lb 13oz)
Cinnamon	1 teaspoon	1½ teaspoons	1½ teaspoons	2 teaspoons	2 teaspoons	2½ teaspoons	3 teaspoons
Mixed spice	1 teaspoon	1½ teaspoons	1½ teaspoons	2 teaspoons	2 teaspoons	2½ teaspoons	3 teaspoons
Brandy	8 tablespoons	10 tablespoons	12 tablespoons	14 tablespoons	16 tablespoons	18 tablespoons	20 tablespoons
Approx baking time	2 hrs 30mins	3 hrs	3 hrs 15mins	3 hrs 30mins	3 hrs 30 mins	4 hrs 15 mins	5 hrs

Method

one Chop the cherries in half and place in a bowl with the mixed peel and the mixed fruit. Add the juice and zest of the oranges and half the quantity of brandy. Stir well. Leave overnight to soak.

two Preheat the oven to 150ºC (300ºF/Gas Mark 2)

three Line the sides and bottom of your tin (see page 12). If it is larger than an 20cm (8in) round or 18cm (7in) square, wrap newspaper around the outside as well.

four Cream together the butter and sugar until they are thoroughly mixed.

five Add the eggs one at a time.

six Sift in the flour and the spices.

seven Mix in the fruit mixture and stir well.

eight Transfer the cake mixture into your tin, smooth the top of the mixture and place into the middle of the oven. Bake for the guide time listed in the recipe.

nine Once out of the oven, leave the cake to cool in the tin.

ten After baking, drizzle the cake with the remaining brandy.

eleven Wrap the cake in cling film and store in an airtight container until required.

Chocolate fudge cake

ROUND	15cm (6in)	18cm (7in)	20cm (8in)	22cm (9in)	25cm (10in)	28cm (11in)	30cm (12in)
SQUARE	12cm (5in)	15cm (6in)	18cm (7in)	20cm (8in)	22cm (9in)	25cm (10in)	28cm (11in)
Margarine or butter	110g (4oz)	130g (4½oz)	190g (6½oz)	220g (8oz)	250g (9oz)	400g (14oz)	440g (15½oz)
Dark chocolate	110g (4oz)	130g (4½oz)	190g (6½oz)	220g (8oz)	250g (9oz)	400g (14oz)	440g (15½oz)
Instant coffee	2 teaspoons	3 teaspoons	4 teaspoons	6 teaspoons	8 teaspoons	12 teaspoons	2½ tablespoons
Water	80ml (2¾ floz)	95ml (3 floz)	140ml (5 floz)	160ml (5½ floz)	180ml (6 floz)	290ml (10 floz)	320ml (11 floz)
Self-raising flour	65g (2oz)	75g (2½oz)	110g (4oz)	125g (4½oz)	150g (5oz)	250g (9oz)	280g (10oz)
Plain flour	65g (2oz)	75g (2½oz)	110g (4oz)	125g (4½oz)	150g (5oz)	250g (9oz)	280g (10oz)
Cocoa powder	25g (1oz)	30g (1oz)	40g (1½oz)	50g (1½oz)	60g (2oz)	90g (3oz)	110g (4oz)
Bicarbonate of soda	¼ teaspoon	¼ teaspoon	¼ teaspoon	½ teaspoon	½ teaspoon	¾ teaspoon	1 teaspoon
Caster sugar	240g (8½oz)	300g (10½oz)	420g (15oz)	480g (1lb 1oz)	550g (1lb 3oz)	860g (1lb 14oz)	960g (2lb 2oz)
Eggs	2	2	3	4	4	7	8
Vegetable oil	4 teaspoons	5 teaspoons	6 teaspoons	7 teaspoons	8 teaspoons	2½ tablespoons	3 tablespoons
Sour cream	60ml (2 floz)	70ml (2½ floz)	95ml (3 floz)	110ml (3½ floz)	125ml (4 floz)	200ml (6½ floz)	220ml (7 floz)
Approx baking time	1 hr 5 mins	1 hr 20 mins	1 hr 30 mins	1 hr 40 mins	1 hr 45 mins	2 hrs 15 mins	2 hrs 30 mins

Method

one Preheat the oven to 160ºC (315ºF/Gas Mark 2–3).

two Line the sides and base of the tin (see page 12).

three Gently melt the butter, chocolate, coffee and water in a pan on a low heat.

four Sift the dry ingredients (flours, cocoa and bicarbonate of soda) into a mixing bowl. Add the sugar.

five In a separate bowl, combine the eggs, oil and sour cream.

six Pour the egg mix and chocolate mix into the dry ingredients and mix well.

seven Pour into the cake tin and place in the middle of the oven.

eight Bake for the guide time listed in the recipe or until a skewer inserted into the centre comes out clean.

nine Remove from the oven and leave the cake to cool in its tin.

Cup & US measurements

If you prefer to use cup measurements, please use the following conversions. (Note: 1 tablespoon = 15ml, except for Australian tablespoons which are 20ml):

butter
1 tablespoon = 15g (½ oz),
2 tablespoons = 25g (1oz),
1 stick = 100g (3½oz),
1 cup = 225g (8oz)

caster (superfine) sugar
2 tablespoons = 25g (1oz),
1 cup = 200g (7oz)

soft brown sugar
1 cup = 115g (4oz)

liquid
1 cup = 250ml (9 floz),
½ cup = 125ml (4 floz)

flour
1 cup = 150g (5oz)

desiccated (dry, unsweetened, shredded)
4 tablespoons = 25g (1oz),
1 cup = 75g (2½oz)

dried fruit
1 cup = 225g (8oz) currants, or 150g (5oz) raisins, or 175g (6oz) sultanas (golden raisins)

glacé (candied) cherries
1 cup = 225g (8oz)

Cake Fillings and Icings

A delicious filling makes a cake taste wonderful. Let the flavour of your cake help you decide what this should be, for example a cream cheese filling goes well with carrot cake and a classic buttercream and raspberry jam filling is perfect for a vanilla sponge. And then there is the icing. Here I describe the different types I use.

Buttercream

A buttercream is used to sandwich together two vanilla sponge cakes and to fill a chocolate or carrot cake.

Materials and equipment

500g (1lb 2oz)
    salted butter
1kg (2lb 3oz)
    sifted icing sugar
2 teaspoons
vanilla extract

(quantities for filling a three-tiered cake)

one Cream the butter until the colour goes a little lighter.

two Sift the icing sugar and thoroughly mix with the butter.

three Add a little milk if required to make a smooth consistency.

four Use on your cake following the steps for Levelling and Filling on page 21.

There are lots of other fillings you can use as well. For example, if you are making a lemon cake, try spreading a layer of lemon curd for the filling and make some lemon drizzle to go on top. I use Duchy Original Lemon Curd for a beautifully zesty flavour and pour caster sugar mixed with lemon juice over my sponge.

Buttercream can also be used as an icing (see White Chocolate Roses, page 80).

Buttercream variations

A traditional vanilla sponge is filled with simple buttercream and jam, but you can use chocolate or orange instead. Be creative with your taste buds and think about what flavours work with each other. For example, a chocolate filling works equally well in an orange cake and an almond cake.

Add the following ingredients to the basic buttercream recipe opposite:

Citrus – the rind and a little juice of 2–3 lemons or oranges.

Chocolate – 175g (6oz) melted plain chocolate.

Coffee – espresso or concentrated instant coffee, 5 tablespoons.

Cream cheese frosting – add full fat cream cheese and the zest of a lemon.

Icing

There are three main types of icing I use to create my designs:

Sugarpaste

Also known as fondant icing, this soft pliable icing is used to cover cakes ready for decorating. When mixed with flowerpaste it becomes a good modelling icing.

Flowerpaste

This is used mainly for handmade sugar flowers but is ideal for any delicate sugarcraft work that requires the strength of a hard setting paste. It's perfect for flowers, bows and frills as it can be rolled out very thinly. It can be purchased from sugarcraft shops either in a small block or as a powder which is mixed with water.

Royal icing

Royal icing (left) is a wet mixture of egg whites (or albumen) and icing sugar which sets extremely hard. It's used for piping details such as flower centres or a snail trail onto cakes and also as a sugar glue for attaching decorations (see also page 28).

Preparing Cakes for Icing

There are a few handy cake making techniques you need to know when getting your cake ready for icing. They will help you make every surface on your cake flat, smooth and level, a flawless blank canvas ready for you to create your design.

Covering cakeboards

An iced cakeboard makes an excellent foundation for both single and multi-tiered cakes. It also provides another surface which can be incorporated into the design.

Materials and equipment

Thick cakeboard

Sugarpaste (see below for quantities)

Icing smoother

Rolling pin

Small sharp knife

Small paintbrush

Quantity guide for covering cake boards (round or square)

Size of board	20cm (8in)	23cm (9in)	25cm (10in)	28cm (11in)	30cm (12in)	33cm (13in)	35.5cm (14in)	38cm (15in)	41cm (16in)
Approx quantity of sugarpaste	625g (1lb 6oz)	725g (1lb 9¾oz)	825g (1lb 13oz)	850g (1lb 14oz)	875g (1lb 15oz)	900g (2lb)	925g (2lb ½oz)	925g (2lb ½oz)	1kg (2lb 3oz)

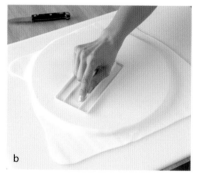

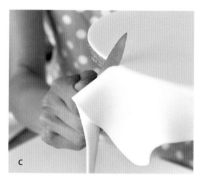

one Brush the cake board with a wet paintbrush, moistening the whole board without adding too much water.

two Roll out the sugarpaste about 3mm (⅛in) thick. Hold the board above the rolled out icing to check it will cover all of it.

three Roll the icing around the rolling pin, lift up and lay onto the wet cake board (**a**).

four Use the icing smoother to finish off, going over the board in a circular motion (**b**).

five Holding the board in one hand, use the sharp knife to trim the excess sugarpaste all round, keeping the knife flush with the edge of the board (**c**).

six Allow to dry overnight.

Levelling and filling

It's very important to make your cake level before you start decorating, especially if you are adding tiers. For best results, use a small spirit level to check you've got it right rather than simply judging by eye.

one Work out what height your cake should be and mark it ready for trimming. Measure with a ruler to ensure it will be the same height all round (**a**).

two Trim the dome from the top of the cake using a sharp knife to make a flat surface (**b**).

three Place the cake on a board and spread with a generous layer of buttercream, then some jam if required. Gently place the second half of the cake on top, checking it is straight (**c**).

four Use the spirit level to check that the cake is flat. If it still needs levelling, add small amounts of sugarpaste icing (each about the size of a small marble) under the cake to raise one side to the right level.

tip If you are worried about cake crumbs getting caught up in the buttercream, coat the cake in a really thin layer of buttercream to start with and place it in the fridge to set. This will act as a seal, so you can add more buttercream to the cake without the risk of getting crumbs everywhere!

Icing Cakes

Applying two coats of icing to your cake will give a really smooth finish and provide the stability necessary for stacking tiers on top of each other. You can use different flavours for the under and top icing. For example, you can under ice a sponge cake in chocolate sugarpaste or marzipan like a fruitcake, if you wish. Again, the flavour of your cake will guide you.

Under icing

It's worth taking care over the under icing on your cake. The smoother the finish you can achieve at this stage, the easier it will be to add the top icing afterwards.

Materials

Cake

Thin cake board the same size
   as the cake

Pastry brush

Apricot glaze/seedless jam

Icing sugar

Sugarpaste (see below
   right for quantities)

Rolling pin

Icing smoother

Sharp knife

a

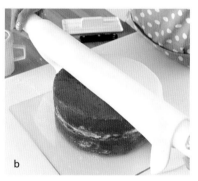

b

c

tip If your glaze or jam has been in the fridge or is a little thick, put some in a bowl in the microwave for about 20 seconds. This will melt the glaze and make it easier to spread.

one Brush the cake with the glaze or jam and set aside (**a**).

two Roll out the sugarpaste or marzipan about 5mm (³/₁₆in) thick and large enough to cover the cake.

three Roll the icing around the rolling pin, lift up and lay onto the cake (**b**).

four Smooth the top and sides of the cake with your hands and an icing smoother to press the icing down onto the cake and form a cutting line (**c**).

five Trim the excess icing around the bottom of the cake with the sharp knife. Allow to dry over night.

Top icing

The top icing is added in the same way as the under icing, except that water is used instead of glaze. Allow yourself plenty of time to ensure you get a perfect finish.

a

b

one Place the under iced cake onto a board and brush with a little water. Moisten the whole cake without making it too wet.

two Dust a work surface with icing sugar, and knead the sugarpaste on it until smooth.

three Roll out the icing 5mm ($^3/_{16}$ in) thick, large enough to cover the whole cake.

four Using the rolling pin, lay the icing over the cake as before.

five Smooth the top and the sides with your hands and an icing smoother (**a**).

six Trim the excess icing around the cake with the sharp knife (**b**).

seven Use a little sugarpaste glue (water and sugarpaste mixed well) or royal icing to stick the cake onto an iced cake board.

tip If you spy any air bubbles caught between the two layers of icing, carefully insert a clean pin to smooth the air out.

Quantity guides

Use these simple guides to calculate the quantity of sugarpaste and marzipan you will need when under icing and top icing your cake.

tip If you are an experienced cakemaker, you may prefer to use one coat of icing on a single tiered cake. The icing should be about 7mm (¼in) thick.

For under icing cakes:

Size of cake (round or square)	15cm (6in)	18cm (7in)	20cm (8in)	23cm (9in)	25cm (10in)	28cm (11in)	30cm (12in)	33cm (13in)	35.5cm (14in)
Approx quantity of sugarpaste or marzipan	650g (1lb 7oz)	700g (1lb 8¾oz)	825g (1lb 13oz)	1kg (2lb 3oz)	1.25kg (2lb 12oz)	1.5 kg (3lb 5oz)	1.75kg (3lb 13¾oz)	2kg (4lb 6½oz)	2.5kg (5lb 8oz)

For top icing cakes:

Size of cake (round or square)	15cm (6in)	18cm (7in)	20cm (8in)	23cm (9in)	25cm (10in)	28cm (11in)	30cm (12in)	33cm (13in)	35.5cm (14in)
Approx quantity of sugarpaste	750g (1lb 10oz)	900g (2lb)	1kg (2lb 3oz)	1.25kg (2lb 12oz)	1.75kg (3lb 13¾oz)	1.85kg (4lb 1¼oz)	2.25kg (4lb 15oz)	2.50kg (5lb 8oz)	3kg (6lb 10oz)

Assembling Tiered Cakes

There are various ways you can assemble the tiers on a cake, all of which include the use of dowels. These are made of plastic or wood and are specially designed to prevent each tier from sinking into the one underneath. Here are the two methods I use for tiered designs.

Stacking cakes

In this technique, which is also known as American Style stacking, plastic cake making dowels are pushed into the cake directly below where the next tier will go, enabling you to stack your tiers securely.

Materials for a three tiered cake

One 15cm (6in), one, 20cm (8in) and one, 25cm (10in) under and top iced cake tier, each mounted on a thin cake board the same size as the cake

Iced thick cake board (see page 20)

Royal icing (see page 28)

12 plastic dowels

Small hacksaw/ serrated knife

Pencil

Palette knife

Scriber needle

a

b

one Spread a small amount of royal icing onto the iced base board and place the largest tier centrally onto the board.

two Take a thin cake board, the same size as the next tier, and place it centrally on top of the bottom tier. Using a scriber needle, score the cake around the board. This helps you to position the dowels and tiers (**a**).

three Insert a dowel into the centre of this tier and make a mark on the dowel to show the height of the cake.

four Remove the dowel and, using the hacksaw or knife, cut the dowel about 1mm (^{1}/$_{16}$in) above the marked line (**b**).

five Cut a further six dowels exactly the same size using the cut dowel as a measure. It's very important that all the dowels are the same size (**c**).

six Push a dowel into the centre of the cake, then insert six more in a circle around it, staying inside the scored line (**d**).

seven Spread a small amount of royal icing on the centre of the cake. Using both hands, carefully place the next tier on top, using the scored line as a guide for positioning the cake board (**e**).

eight If you are making a three tiered cake, repeat these steps with the top tier using five dowels this time.

Blocking cakes with fresh flowers

Fresh flowers look stunning on a cake. They can be pushed into polystyrene blocks and stacked between cake tiers. I use this technique for the Champagne Bubbles wedding cake on page 36.

Materials

Three, under and top iced cake tiers, each mounted on a larger iced and ribboned cake board (see pages 20 and 29)

Two, 5cm (2in) thick polystyrene blocks, each 2.5cm (1in) smaller than the cake tier it will support

12 plastic dowels

Pencil

Small hacksaw/ serrated knife

Scriber needle

a

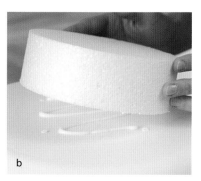
b

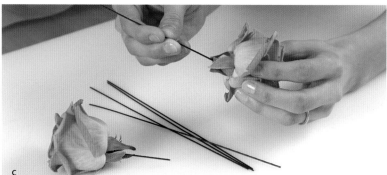
c

one Place the largest polystyrene block in the centre of the bottom cake tier and score round it using the scriber needle (**a**).

two Insert a dowel in the centre of the cake and mark it to show the height of the cake. Remove the dowel and, using the hacksaw or knife, cut it about 1mm ($^1/_{16}$in) above the marked line.

three Cut a further six dowels to the exact same size using the cut dowel as a measure. It is very important to ensure that all the dowels are the same size (see steps four and five on pages 24–25).

four Push a dowel down into the centre of the cake and insert another six in a circle around it, inside the scored line.

five Spread a little royal icing in the centre of the cake and stick the correct size polystyrene block on top (**b**).

six To prepare the fresh roses for blocking, take small lengths of thick florists wire and insert one in the end of each rose head (**c**).

d

e

seven Carefully push the prepared roses into the polystyrene block (**d**).

eight Attach the next tier and polystyrene block in the same way, following steps one to seven (**e**).

nine Spread more royal icing over the polystyrene block and attach the top tier.

You can use a beautiful range of fresh flowers to add a simply stunning finish to your cake.

Finishing Touches

Icing can be used effectively to add that special finishing touch to your cake. Here I explain a few of my favourite techniques.

Royal icing

I use royal icing to create all of the delicate sugar pipe work and as a sugar glue to stick cake tiers together. Once made, the icing will last in an airtight container for up to seven days. You will only require a small amount of royal icing for each project.

Use 1 medium egg white to 300g (10½oz) sugar. Beat together in a mixing bowl until smooth and the icing forms peaks. If the consistency is a little dry, add a few drops of water.

To make a piping bag for royal icing

one Fold some greaseproof paper about 33cm (13in) square in half to make a triangle and place on a table with the point facing you.

two Take the right-hand corner and fold around your hand to make a cone.

three Fold the left-hand corner all the way around the cone to meet the other side.

four Secure your piping bag by folding over the corner to the inside.

five Cut off the tip about 1cm (½in) from the end, and slip on your piping nozzle.

tip Avoid overfilling a piping bag in case it leaks from the top. Fill the bag no more than two-thirds full. And don't forget to add the nozzle!

Snail trail

This pattern is usually piped along the line where the cake meets the cake board. You can also pipe icing around the top of a cake, as I did on the Candy Stripes design on page 118.

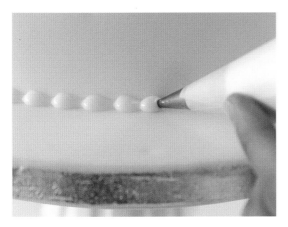

one Hold the piping bag at a 60º angle to your cake, the nozzle just touching the icing.

two Make a pearl of icing, and ease off the pressure as you move the piping bag to the right to make a tail. Pipe the next pearl over the tail of the previous pearl to make a continuous line.

three Continue all round the cake in this way, joining the last pearl neatly to the first one.

Using ribbon on cakes and boards

Instead of a snail trail you might choose to use a satin ribbon. This can often be a nice way of incorporating colour on a simply iced cake.

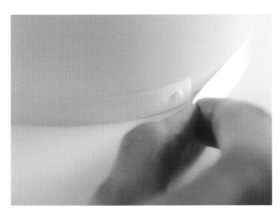

To ribbon a cake

one Cut your ribbon just longer than the circumference of the cake. Wrap it round the base.

two With a little royal icing, stick one end of the ribbon to the cake, apply more icing to the upper side and stick the other end of the ribbon down on top.

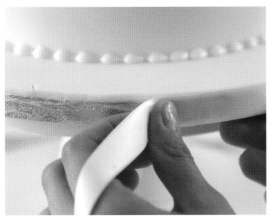

To ribbon a board

one Put the board onto a turntable and run all round the edge with an adhesive stick.

two Without cutting the ribbon from the roll, stick the end to the board.

three Wind the ribbon all the way round the edge, sticking it down as you go.

four When you get back to the end, cut the ribbon, leaving extra to stick it down on top.

Buttercream is the perfect finishing touch for a freshly baked chocolate treat.

Cupcakes and Mini Cakes

Cupcakes really are a favourite any-time treat for kids, big and little! They are so simple to create, take no time to bake and cool in minutes. I often make more mixture than I need to for a large cake so I can include some sneaky cupcakes for tea. Mini cakes take a little longer, but can be a real showstopper. They're perfect for a very special occasion.

Cupcakes

Any of the recipes on pages 14–17 (except for the fruit cake) work perfectly as cupcakes, especially the chocolate fudge cake and carrot cake which are both very moist cakes. You will get around 12 cupcakes from an 18cm (7in) round recipe.

Materials

Muffin tin
Muffin paper cases
Buttercream (see page 18)

one Preheat oven to 160ºC/325° F/ Gas Mark 3. Line a muffin tin with muffin paper cases.

two Make your cake mixture using your chosen recipe from pages 14–17. Fill each muffin case about two-thirds full. Bake the cakes for about 20 minutes until they bounce back on touch.

three Leave to cool for a few minutes and turn out onto a cooling rack.

four Smooth buttercream over each cake as a frosting.

Mini cakes

You can make mini cakes either with individual mini cake trays or by baking a slab cake about 5cm (2in) deep and cutting out rounds with a 5cm (2in) pastry cutter. (This method leaves plenty of leftover cake to sample!) Individual trays are best for ensuring your mini cakes are all the same size and height.

Any of the recipes on pages 14–17 are suitable for mini cakes. Grease the individual trays well and fill each one about two-thirds. You will get 25 mini cakes from a 30cm (12in) square tin recipe.

Icing mini cakes

Iced mini cakes really do look special. They are iced in the same way as a larger cake but only need a single coat. Festive mini cakes can be under iced with marzipan.

Materials

Sugarpaste, 2.5kg (5lb 8oz) for
    25 mini cakes
Apricot glaze or seedless jam
Rolling pin
Icing smoother

one When the cakes are cooled, cut each one in half and fill with buttercream and jam as required (see page 18).

two Brush each mini cake with apricot glaze or jam.

three Roll out the icing about 5mm ($^3/_{16}$in) thick and cut a 14cm (5½in) square for each cake.

four Place a square over each cake and smooth down with your hands and an icing smoother. Trim the excess with a sharp knife and set on a tray lined with greaseproof paper (**a**).

five Allow the mini cakes to harden for a couple of hours. Cut a length of satin ribbon to fit around each cake and attach with a little royal icing (see page 29) (**b**).

Use lashings of buttercream with your favourite jam to complement your chosen recipe.

Pastels

Champagne Bubbles

Here's a wonderful romantic wedding cake that's traditional in shape, yet contemporary in design. The lines of piped bubbles are easy to create, and the lustre finish provides an elegant touch. Fresh flowers make a popular alternative to sugar flowers as they are easily matched to the bride's floral theme. Dreamy pink roses set between each tier give the cake extra height and transform it into a beautiful centrepiece.

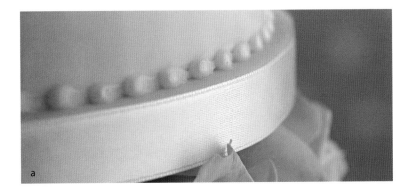

a

one Add a pin prick amount of cream food colouring to your royal icing to turn it a light shade of ivory to match your cake.

two Make two piping bags to hold your royal icing and add the no.1.5 and no.3 nozzles (see page 28). Using the no.3 nozzle, snail trail around the bottom of each cake (see page 29) (**a**).

Materials

One, 15cm (6in), one, 20cm (8in) and one, 25cm (10in) round ivory iced cake, each set onto a round ivory iced and ribboned cake board, 3cm (1in) larger than the cake (see pages 14–27)

One, 35.5cm (14in) round ivory iced and ribboned cake board

Cream food colouring

White royal icing (see page 28)

Snowflake lustre

One, 10cm (4in) and one, 15cm (6in) round, 2in deep polystyrene block

About 30 large roses

Equipment

No.3 and No.1.5 icing nozzles

Nine plastic dowels

Florists wire

Small paintbrush

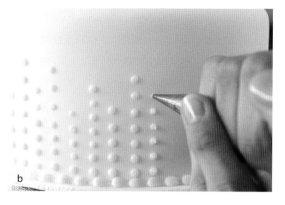

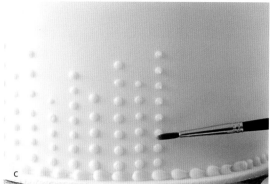

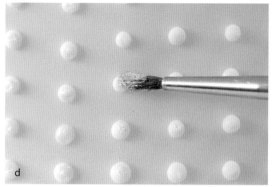

tip If you find it hard to pipe in a straight line, lightly score a line onto the cake first using a scriber needle or pin and a ruler. Pipe the small dots up this line, then use it as a guide for where the next line should go.

three Using the no.1.5 piping bag, pipe the first line of tiny dots of icing onto the side of one of the cakes. Start just above the snail trail and finish two-thirds of the way up (**b**).

four Add five or six more lines of dots, spacing them equally and varying the length of each one to make a delicate pattern. Stop and dab down the sugar peaks with a wet brush before adding some more (**c**).

five Cover each cake with lines of dots in this way and set aside to dry. Then apply snowflake lustre to the sugar bubbles with a small dry dusting brush (**d**).

six Assemble the tiers following the instructions for blocking cakes with fresh flowers on page 26, inserting the polystyrene blocks between the tiers.

tip Make sure that the tiers are centred when you place them on top of each other. You may find it helpful if someone stands on the other side of the cake to check for you.

seven Cut off the rose heads and gently insert a length of thick wire into each flower so you can push it into the polystyrene block (**e**).

e

Using fresh roses adds a magical touch to a cake for such a special occasion. Their lovely scent will be an extra surprise for the wedding party when they see the cake for the first time.

This beautiful centrepiece will impress all your wedding guests. Simply choose flowers that co-ordinate with your colour scheme.

Simply Inspired...

Piped sugar bubbles will add an elegant touch to any cake, whatever its size, shape... or colour! If your scheme is pink and you fancy something a little brighter at your celebration, why not go all the way and design your cake to match? It makes a gorgeous pink dream.

Rose pink

You can simply push fresh flowers into the top of the cake instead of displaying them between the tiers. Here, red roses contrast beautifully with the shade of pink chosen for the cake, and a matching ribbon bow trailing across the cake adds a stunning final touch to this design.

tip If you want the colour of your champagne bubbles to be an exact match, try using some of the sugarpaste left over from icing the cake instead of royal icing. This can be mixed into a paste with a little water.

Butterfly Kisses

Materials

One, 15cm (6in) and one,
23cm (9in) round white
iced cake, stacked and
set onto a 30.5cm (12in)
round iced and ribboned
cake board (see pages
14–25), or a glass plate

White flowerpaste, 150g (5oz)

Royal icing (see page 28)

Ruby, grape violet, spruce
green and melon food
colouring

30 white stamens for the
butterfly antennae

Equipment

Butterfly cutter or template
on page 134

Blossom ejector cutter,
13mm (1/2in)

Daisy cutter, 14mm (1/2in)
and 19mm (3/4in)

No.3 and No.2 icing nozzles

Small leaf icing nozzle

Bone tool and pins

Scriber needle

Flower foam pad

Stay fresh plastic mat

Small rolling pin

Thin silver chain or necklace

Folded piece of card

White wire, 24-gauge

This Butterfly Cake is one of my earliest designs. It was inspired by the book *Brambly Hedge Summer Story*. This tale, about the wedding of two small field mice, really captured my imagination as a child. Whenever I think of it now, it brings back happy memories of summer days, picnics, country fetes and weddings. The cake is decorated with swags of small sugar flowers and fluttering sugar butterflies. Simply summer!

a

b

one Divide the white flowerpaste into three balls and mix with the food colouring to make light pink, soft pink and soft lilac, adding a tiny amount of colouring to each one. Roll out the balls about 1mm (1/16in) thick on a large board so that you have a colour palette in front of you. Dust them with snowflake lustre to make the icing shimmer and place the icing under the stay fresh mat to prevent it drying out (**a**).

two Cut out the flowers using the two different size daisy cutters and the blossom ejector cutter. Cut 25 of each colour with each type of cutter, making a total of 225 flowers. When using the blossom ejector cutter, form the flower by ejecting onto the foam pad (**b**).

43

tip You can use a cereal box or a couple of old birthday cards to make your butterfly former.

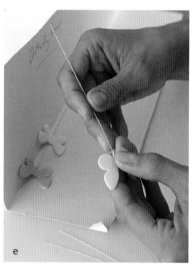

tip Remember to make some extra flowers to go on matching cupcakes (see page 47).

three Place the flowers on a foam pad and, using the small end of the bone tool, smooth each petal towards the centre until the tip curls up (**c**).

four Now cut out 15 butterflies from the same icing, five in each colour. Take nine of the butterflies and shape using the folded piece of card (**d**).

five Cut six lengths of wire, dip them in water and gently push them into the centre of the other six butterflies. Shape them with the folded card as before (**e**).

six Measure the circumference of each cake tier and cut a length of greaseproof paper to go round it. Fold the length for the top tier into four sections and the length for the base tier into six sections. Wrap them around the cakes, securing them with a pin. Mark each fold in the paper with a scriber needle or pin, positioning your marks about 1.5cm down from the top of the cake (**f**).

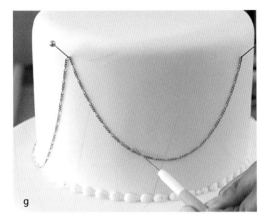
g

h

i

j

seven Remove the paper. Pin one end of the necklace to one of the marks on the cake. Draw the necklace up to the next mark to create a swag about 2.5cm (1in) from the base of the cake. Hold the necklace in place with a pin then, using a scriber needle or pin, score the side of the cake following the line of the necklace. Continue around the cake and repeat on the other tier ready for adding the flowers (**g**).

eight Make two piping bags, fill with royal icing and add the icing nozzles (see page 28). Using the no.3 nozzle, snail trail around the bottom of each cake (see page 29). Use the no.2 nozzle to fix the flowers to the cake. Arrange them in alternate shapes and colours along the lines marked on the cake (**h**).

nine Using the same piping bag, pipe the centre of each flower. Use a small brush and some water to dab down the icing peaks when you complete each swag (**i**).

ten Mix a small amount of spruce green food colouring with some royal icing, and add a tiny amount of melon yellow to create a fresher shade of green. Fill a piping bag with this icing and the leaf nozzle. Pipe leaves on both sides of the flowers on each swag (**j**).

k

l

eleven Using the white royal icing with the no.2 nozzle, pipe the body down the centre of each butterfly and leave to dry (**k**).

twelve Push two small stamens about 1cm (½in) long into the top of the butterfly body for the antennae. When dry, stick each butterfly on to the side of the cake using a little royal icing (**l**).

tip If you want to find the exact centre of the top tier to push in your wired butterflies, measure with a ruler and mark with a small cross beforehand.

m

thirteen Push the butterflies on wires into the top of the cake and add a couple of extra flowers around the base of the wires (**m**).

Simply Inspired...

Sugar flowers and butterflies make the perfect decoration for cupcakes topped with buttercream. You can add as many toppers as you want, or even create your own beautiful butterfly fairy cakes using large butterfly cutters.

Teatime fancies

Make your cupcakes and buttercream as explained on pages 18 and 30. Cover the top of each cupcake with buttercream, smoothing it with a knife before pushing your decorations gently into the surface. I used three flowers and a butterfly on mine, but you can vary this.

tip Cupcakes are ideal for trying out new ideas or themes for the first time. The pink and mauve flowers and butterflies will look completely different (but just as special) on coffee or chocolate buttercream.

Dotty About You

I love incorporating feathers in my cake designs. They are such a fun decoration to use, and make a huge impact. Here I combine feathers with icing polka dots in soft pastel shades to create a stylish design for a birthday or other celebration cake. The polka dots are easy to make from coloured sugarpaste. What a wonderful way to let someone know you're dotty about them!

Materials

One, 15cm (6in) and one, 25cm (10in) round white iced cake, stacked and set onto a 38cm (15in) round iced and ribboned cake board (see pages 14–25)
White sugarpaste, 250g (9oz)
Mint green, baby blue, pink, melon and grape violet food colouring
Snowflake lustre
Feathers

Equipment

No.3 icing nozzle
White florists tape
Small paintbrush

a

b

one Divide the sugarpaste into five and mix with the food colourings to make a yellow, blue, pink, mauve and green ball. Only use a tiny amount of colouring at a time to create each pastel shade (**a**).

two Roll out each icing colour on a large board about 2mm (1/16in) thick and arrange them into a colour palette. Dust each colour with snowflake lustre to make the icing shimmer (**b**).

c

d

tip To create a different theme for your cake, try using small star, heart or flower cutters instead of circles. You can use any size and type of cutter for this.

e

three Cut out the polka dots using the wide end of your no.3 nozzle (**c**).

four Remove the dots from the nozzle, by blowing through the other end (**d**).

five Make a piping bag, fill with royal icing and add the no.3 nozzle (see page 28). Snail trail around the bottom of each cake tier (see page 29).

six Arrange the polka dots randomly across the cake, adding one colour at a time to ensure you use an equal number of each shade. Dab a little water onto the back of each polka dot with the paintbrush first (**e**).

seven Wrap the ends of your feathers tightly together with white florists tape, covering about 2.5cm (1in) with tape. Slowly and carefully push the taped end into the centre of the top tier of the cake. To prevent the icing cracking, use a skewer to make a small hole first (**f**).

You can adapt your cake to suit a particular taste or occasion by using a different colour way – perhaps pale pink or pale blue for a christening cake or bright colours for a fun birthday design.

Simply Inspired...

Mini cakes are brilliant in creating the essence of a design in a fun and stylish way. They make fabulous gifts or favours for guests to take home from a party. They look so pretty displayed together on a stand or table, ready to be handed around later. See pages 32–33 for how to make and ice mini cakes, and the recipes on pages 14–17.

Ribbon fancy

If you're really pressed for time, simply tie a ribbon bow around a plain iced mini cake. This makes a stylish instant embellishment and the perfect contrast to the polka dot cakes, especially if you choose ribbon in matching pastel shades to continue the colour theme.

Box of delights

A clear presentation box is an excellent way to show off your cake decorating skills and makes a special finishing touch for a party gift or favour. You can pop a delicious mini cake inside and tie on an organza ribbon to ensure you can still admire the box's pretty contents.

Blue Buttons

My designs tend to be quite pink and girly, so I thought I'd better put one in for the boys! The sugar buttons and gorgeous patchwork teddy on this cake are fun and easy to make. The piped 'stitching' on the teddy patch gives an authentic handmade look. This theme continues around the side of the cake with blue sugar buttons piped to look as though they are sewn on, too. Scattered blue sugar stars complete this effective yet simple design.

Materials

One, 33cm (13in) round white iced cake, set onto a 38cm (15in) round, white, iced and ribboned cake board (see pages 14–23)

White sugarpaste, 250g (9oz)

Flowerpaste, 50g (1¾oz)

Royal icing (see page 28)

Baby blue and brown food colouring

Equipment

Small star cutter, 20mm (¾in)

Small circle cutters for buttons, two sizes

No.3 and No.1 icing nozzles

Rolling pin

Scriber needle

Small paintbrush

one Make a piping bag, add some royal icing and the no.3 nozzle, and snail trail around the base of the cake (see page 28).

two Mix up 200g (8oz) sugarpaste with a tiny amount of baby blue food colouring to make it a pale blue shade. Wrap in clingfilm and set aside.

three Trace the teddy bear template on page 134 onto tracing paper. Transfer the image onto a thin piece of card and cut this out.

four Roll out half of the pale blue icing about 2mm (¹/₁₆in) thick. Place the card teddy on top and cut out the shape with a sharp knife. Dab a small amount of water onto the back of the bear with a paintbrush and place it in the centre of the cake (**a**).

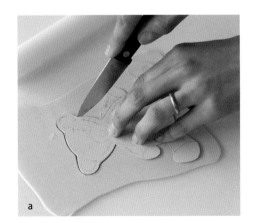

a

55

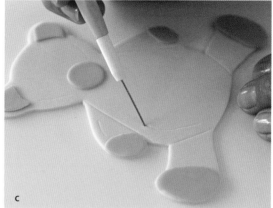

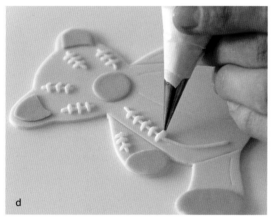

tip You can incorporate the iced cake board into your design by adding some of the decorations from the cake. Here, the blue stars cover both the cake and board.

five Trace the teddy bear's details (paws, feet, nose and ears) and transfer them onto card as before. Cut out these shapes. Take a small amount of the leftover pale blue icing and mix in a little more food colouring to turn it a darker shade of blue. Roll out the icing about 2mm (¹/₁₆in) thick and cut out the shapes. Stick them onto the teddy bear using a little water (**b**).

six Using a scriber needle or a pin, score lines onto the teddy bear's body where you want the stitches to be piped (**c**).

seven Half fill a piping bag with white royal icing and the no.1 nozzle (see page 28). Pipe the stitches following the marked lines. Dab any icing peaks that form with a wet paintbrush (**d**).

eight Mix a tiny amount of white sugarpaste with brown food colouring for the eyes, nose and mouth. Make three tiny balls for the eyes and nose, and a sausage shape for the mouth. Attach to the teddy with a little water.

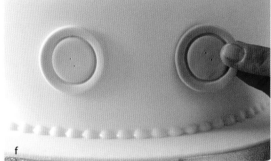

nine Combine the flowerpaste with the remaining 50g (1¾oz) of sugarpaste, and divide into two balls. Mix with baby blue food colouring to match the two shades of blue on the teddy. Roll out about 3–4mm (1/8in) thick. Cut out the buttons with circle cutters. Position a smaller circle cutter over each button and press lightly to indent the button detail. Mark the centre of each button with the scriber needle to make the thread holes (**e**).

ten Pipe a little icing onto the back of each button using the no.1 nozzle and stick it to the side of the cake. Space the buttons evenly apart (**f**).

eleven Pipe the stitches onto the buttons using the no.1 nozzle. Dab any icing peaks with a little water (**g**).

twelve Roll out the rest of the pale blue sugarpaste, cut out some stars and stick to the cake with a dab of water.

Simply Inspired...

You can also make a pretty pink buttons cake in the same style for a little girl, decorated with a little posy of flowers and pale pink buttons. This is an ideal first project if you've never tried cake decorating before.

Sugar buttons are so simple to make and look great fun on cupcakes, especially if you mix a range of different styles and colours.

So simple

The flowers on the top of this cake are cut from rolled out sugarpaste coloured a bright shade of pink, using two different size blossom cutters. The flower centres are cut out from sugarpaste with the large end of an icing nozzle and stuck to the cake with a little water. The stems are piped onto the cake in royal icing mixed with spruce green food colouring, from a piping bag fitted with a no.2 nozzle (see page 28). The buttons are made as explained in steps nine and ten on the previous page, using a single shade of pale pink icing.

Materials

One, 25cm (10in) round
   white iced cake
   (see pages 14–23)
White sugarpaste,
   100g (3½oz)
   Flowerpaste, 50g (1¾oz)
White royal icing
   (see page 28)
Spruce green and pink
   food colouring
Blossom cutters, two sizes

Lavender and Hearts

Mini cakes are popular with brides who want a traditional wedding cake with an unusual twist. The little cakes can be displayed in a traditional wedding cake shape on a tiered cake stand, or individually placed next to each guest's place. You can send one to someone who can't be with you on the day. I decorated my mini cakes with piped sprigs of lavender and yellow sugar hearts, and used a larger cake for the top tier.

Materials

One, 15cm (6in) round white iced cake set onto an 20cm (8in) iced and ribboned cake board (see pages 14–23)

One, 25cm (10in), one 30cm (12in) and one, 35.5cm (14in) iced and ribboned cake board (see page 29)

24 white iced mini cakes (see page 32)

White sugarpaste, 100g (3½oz) per mini cake

Royal icing (see page 28)

Grape violet, spruce green and melon yellow food colouring

10mm (¼in) silver satin ribbon

Equipment

Small heart plunger cutter
No.1.5 icing nozzle
Small leaf icing nozzle
Flower foam pad
Stay fresh plastic mat
Bone tool
Scriber needle or pin
Small rolling pin
Small paintbrush
12 white plastic cake pillars

one Wrap silver ribbon around the base of each mini cake and the 15cm (6in) cake for the top tier, securing with royal icing (see page 29) (**a**).

two Mix half of the royal icing with spruce green food colouring and the other half with grape violet food colouring to make the piping colours for the lavender. Add only a tiny amount of colour at a time (**b**).

tip Take your time over stacking the mini cakes. Stand back to check each tier is level before adding the next one.

three Using a scriber needle or pin, score 6–8 vertical lines around the sides of a mini cake. Mark half the cakes in this way (**c**).

four Fill a piping bag (see page 28) with the green icing and the small leaf nozzle, and pipe stems and leaves onto the side of the mini cakes, following the marked lines.

five Fill another piping bag with the grape violet icing and the no.1.5 nozzle, and pipe a line of lavender above each stem. Then pipe small horizontal lines outwards from the central line for the lavender seeds (**d**).

six Mix a tiny amount of melon yellow food colouring with the sugarpaste. Roll out about 1mm ($^1/_{16}$in) thick and dust with snowflake lustre. Cut 16 hearts for each cake using the plunger cutter. Stick them randomly onto the remaining cakes with a little water (**e**).

seven Decorate the top tier with 14 lines of piped lavender, following steps three to five.

eight Display your mini cakes on the iced and ribboned boards on a stand. Stack the tiers using cake pillars. Arrange ten cakes and five pillars on the base tier, followed by eight cakes and four pillars, six cakes and three pillars, and, finally, the top tier.

These little cakes make a big impression, especially when displayed on a tiered stand as a fun alternative to the traditional wedding cake.

Simply Inspired...

If you prefer something a little less formal, make cupcakes instead of mini cakes and decorate them with single large yellow flowers and piped lavender. If you are making the cakes for a party, they will look stunning presented in clear gift boxes.

Materials

Flowerpaste, 50g (1¾oz)

Melon yellow food colouring

Blossom flower cutter

Piping bag with grape violet
   icing and a no.1.5 nozzle
   (see page 62, step five)

Pretty blossoms

Colour a little flowerpaste with some melon yellow food colouring, roll out 1–2mm (¹/₁₆in) thick, cut out your flowers and place them in a supermarket apple tray to form the right shape. Allow to dry overnight, then pipe a little of the royal icing used for the lavender in the middle of the flower. Dab down any peaks with water.

You can make your cupcakes look extra special by using silver muffin cases and tying gift boxes with matching ribbon.

Whites

Wedding Ruffles

When I was searching for my perfect wedding dress, I found a wonderful creation that inspired me to make this cake. The skirt was completely covered in ruffles and the top had beautiful lace embroidery. I think the square cake tiers balance out the round ruffles and give the design stature, making this pure cake couture!

Materials

One, 13cm (5in), one, 18cm (7in), one, 28cm (11in) and one, 35.5cm (14in) square ivory iced cake (see pages 14–23)

One, 46cm (18in) iced and ribboned cake board

Celebration sugarpaste, 150g (5oz)

Flowerpaste, 150g (5oz)

Royal icing (see page 28)

Snowflake lustre

25mm (1in) ivory satin ribbon

Diamantes (optional)

Equipment

One, 20mm (¾in), one, 45mm (1¾in) and one, 65mm (2½in) circle cutter

Small blossom plunger cutter

No.1.5 icing nozzle

Scriber needle

Cocktail stick

Stay fresh mat

Small paintbrush

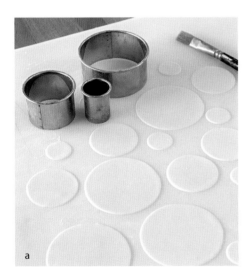

a

one Assemble the four tiers of your cake using dowels as explained on page 24, then wrap ivory ribbon around the base of each tier and secure it as explained on page 29.

two Mix the flowerpaste and sugarpaste and roll out around 2mm (¹/₁₆in) thick.

three Cut out a series of circles, using the three size cutters. Gather up the rest of the icing and wrap in clingfilm. Dust the circles with snowflake lustre (**a**).

tip It's better to apply snowflake lustre after you have cut out the circles because lustred icing can turn a little grey when you mix it back up into a ball.

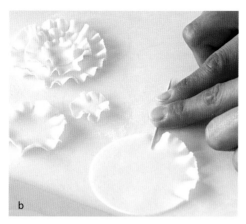

four To make the first ruffle, dust your board with icing sugar and place a large circle on top. Place the end of the cocktail stick over the edge of the circle and roll it back and forth fairly hard so that the icing begins to ruffle up. Work your way around the whole circle in this way, then repeat with a circle in each of the other sizes (**b**).

five Stick the smallest circle in the centre of the middle size circle with a dab of water, then stick this in the centre of the large circle to form a rosette. Wet the back of the rosette and carefully place it onto the side of the cake (**c**).

six Make enough ruffles to cover the sides of the second and fourth tiers of the cake in this way.

seven Trace the flower template on page 134 onto a small square of greaseproof paper. Pin this to the top tier and score the image onto the cake using a scriber needle or pin. Cover the top tier, and the sides of the third tier with a scored flower pattern (**d**).

eight Put royal icing into a piping bag (see page 28) with the no.1.5 nozzle. Pipe over the marked pattern. When you complete each flower, dab down the peaks with a wet paintbrush (**e**).

nine Roll out some of the icing left over from the ruffles, dust with snowflake lustre and cut out some flowers with the blossom cutter. Stick them between the piped flowers with a little water.

ten Decorate the centre of each ruffle and piped flower with a diamante, attaching it with royal icing, or pipe a sugar pearl instead. Dab down the icing peaks with a little water afterwards.

Diamantes add a touch of glamour to the ruffles and piped flowers. You can pipe an icing pearl instead of each gem if you prefer.

Simply Inspired...

tip White ruffles will make a fabulous decoration for cupcakes iced with chocolate buttercream

If you want to give your design even more fru-fru, cover your entire cake in ruffles. The effect will be sensational, whatever size or shape cake you choose, and ruffles work well with any combination of tiers. Here I created a two-tier design using one, 13cm (5in) and one, 23cm (9in) square cake.

Individual ruffles

Delicate ruffles make the ultimate decoration for cupcakes topped with buttercream. To create these little lovelies, bake and ice a series of cupcakes (see pages 30–31), create your ruffles as before and stick one directly onto each cake. Finish off with a small sugar pearl or diamanté.

White Christmas

I love Christmas time and I adore Christmas cake. This sparkling number is a real delight and is so simple to make. Keeping the whole cake white reminds me of a blanket of glistening snow on Christmas morning. You can add colour if you prefer, with red berries or a burgundy ribbon. The result will be just as gorgeous.

Materials

One, 25cm (10in) white iced cake set onto a 33cm (13in) white iced and ribboned cake board (see pages 14–23)
Flowerpaste, 25g (1oz)
Royal icing (see page 28)
Snowflake lustre
White edible glitter
10mm (½in) and 25mm (1in) white satin ribbon

Equipment

Circle cutter, 14cm (5½in)
PME holly plunger cutter
No.1.5 icing nozzle
Small rolling pin
Flower foam pad
Stay fresh plastic mat
Bone tool

a

one Lightly score a circle in the centre of the cake using the circle cutter (**a**).

two Roll out some of the flowerpaste about 1mm (¹/₁₆in) thick, and brush with a little snowflake lustre to make it shimmer.

tip Use a stay fresh plastic mat to keep rolled out icing moist until you need it again.

three Cut out enough holly leaves to fit around the marked circle on the cake. Place them on the foam pad and use the plunger attached to the holly cutter to add veins to each leaf (**b**).

four Use the bone tool to feather the edges of each holly leaf, then set them aside to dry (**c**).

five Shape some small balls of flowerpaste for the berries, brush with a little water and roll in white glitter. Leave to dry (**d**).

e

f

six Arrange the holly leaves and berries on the cake in a garland shape, using the scored circle as a guide. Stick each one down with a dab of royal icing using a piping bag with the no.1.5 nozzle (see page 28) (**e**).

seven Make a small bow with a length of the narrow ribbon and stick at the base of the garland with a little royal icing. Wrap the wider ribbon around the base of the cake (see page 29).

eight Pipe a series of sugar snow-flakes randomly over the cake using the piping bag and no.1.5 nozzle. Dab down the icing peaks with a little water (**f**).

This exquisite design is simple to recreate and will probably inspire you to make your own Christmas cake.

Simply Inspired...

Mini fruit cakes decorated with gold holly leaves and red berries
will add a special touch when you're having a small gathering at
Christmas, especially if you pop them in presentation boxes and
give one to each of your guests. I edged my mini cakes with a
burgundy ribbon for an extra festive feel.

Festive colours

Make your mini cakes following the traditional fruit cake recipe
on page 16, and further advice on page 32. Coat each cake with
first marzipan, then ivory icing. Decorate with holly berries shaped
from bright red flowerpaste and gold painted holly leaves.

> tip For fabulous tasting mini fruit
> cakes, make yours several weeks in
> advance, and soak them in a little brandy
> before icing them.

White Chocolate Roses

Perhaps a little less ornate than some of the other designs in the book, but certainly sweet and simple! I would guess that everybody loves chocolate and this cake really does suit any age or occasion. I've used white chocolate, but the design would work just as well (some might say better!) with milk or dark chocolate curls and roses. Be careful to leave enough curls to use on the cake!

Materials

One, 15cm (6in) and one, 25cm (10in) round, buttercream-filled, un-iced cake (see pages 14–21)
33cm (13in) ivory iced cake board or glass plate
15cm (6in) thin board
Five plastic dowels
Vanilla buttercream (see page 18)
Chocolate curls, two 700g (1lb 8¾oz) packs
White chocolate Cocoform
25mm (1in) ivory satin ribbon

Equipment

Spatula

one Place the 25cm (10in) sponge cake onto the iced cake board or glass plate. Measure the chocolate curls and make sure that the cake is about 1cm (½in) shorter. If necessary, cut your cake to the right size (see levelling cakes on page 21).

two Smooth vanilla butter cream over the top of the cake with the spatula (**a**).

three Spread buttercream part way round the side of the cake and stick chocolate curls to it. Repeat around the rest of the cake, spreading a little buttercream at a time to ensure it doesn't dry out before you get to it (**b**).

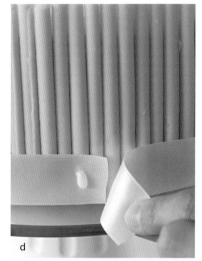

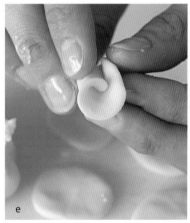

tip Cocoform is a chocolate paste made from pure Belgian chocolate and glucose that's ideal for shaping cake flowers with. For a different effect, try making your roses from milk or dark Cocoform.

four Place the top cake on the 15cm (6in) thin board and cover with buttercream. Insert the dowels in the base tier following the instructions for stacking cakes on page 24. Add the top tier and decorate with chocolate curls as before (**c**).

five Measure the circumference of each tier and cut a ribbon to go round the base of each one, allowing a little extra as well. Secure with royal icing (see page 29) (**d**).

six Take some Cocoform to make the white chocolate roses. Knead it gently until it is pliable. Avoid over kneading or the butter content will start to melt and the icing become sticky. Shape small balls of Cocoform and flatten them out with your fingers to make petals, keeping the edges neat. You will need about six petals per rose.

seven Take a Cocoform petal and curl it around, creating the centre of the rose (**e**).

eight Wrap five further petals around the centre bud to form your rose. For a larger rose, use more petals (**f**).

nine Make enough flowers to fill the gaps remaining on the top and base tier. Push them gently into the buttercream. To raise the roses in the centre of the top tier, place a small round mini cake or more buttercream underneath them.

The white chocolate decorations on this delicious cake are a delight for both the eyes and the tastebuds!

Simply Inspired...

You can use chocolate curls and roses to decorate any cake, whether it's a round, square... or heart-shaped one like this stunning design. Fresh pink roses provide a touch of romance and contrast beautifully with the white chocolate curls on the perfect Valentine's cake.

Chocolate Box

To create this delicious design, a 20cm (8in) square cake was edged with milk chocolate curls and decorated with both white and milk chocolate roses. The board is iced with a chocolate sugarpaste. Try filling this cake with a dark chocolate butter cream and a cherry compote for a perfect black forest treat.

More Simply Inspired...

For stunning and absolutely delicious cupcakes, make some chocolate flavoured cakes, and decorate each one with a layer of piped chocolate buttercream followed by a single white chocolate rose. Place them in a beautiful lined box as the ultimate gift for someone who loves chocolate.

one Make some chocolate flavoured cupcakes following the advice on page 31 and the vanilla sponge recipe on page 14. Make some chocolate buttercream as explained on page 18 (**a**).

two Put some chocolate buttercream in a piping bag (see page 28) with a savoy star-shaped nozzle. Pipe the top of each cupcake, starting on the outside and working round in a circle until you reach the centre (**b**).

three Make a white chocolate rose for each cupcake as explained on pages 82–3 and gently place in the centre of the piped chocolate buttercream (**c**).

Cascading Blossoms

The elegant simplicity makes this one of my most enjoyable cakes. Shaping and attaching sugar flowers is the only technique involved, but it still takes quite a lot of time and concentration to complete this beautiful design. I've made the cake in lots of different colour combinations, but the white on white version remains a favourite.

Materials

One, 15cm (6in) and one, 23cm (9in) round ivory iced cake (see pages 14–23)

One, 30.5cm (12in) ivory iced and ribboned cake board (see page 29)

Flowerpaste, 150g (5oz)

Royal icing (see page 28)

Snowflake lustre

2.5cm (1in) ivory satin ribbon

Equipment

Small flower cutters, three different types

No.1.5 icing nozzle

Flower foam pad

Bone tool

Stay fresh plastic mat

Small paintbrush

a

one Assemble your cake on the iced and ribboned board following the instructions on stacking cakes on page 24. Wrap ivory ribbon around the base of each tier (see page 29).

two Roll out some white flowerpaste about 1mm (1/16in) thick. Brush with a little snowflake lustre and place the icing under a stay fresh mat to prevent it drying out.

three Cut out an equal amount of flowers with each cutter, around 400 in total. Place the flowers on the foam pad and form the petals on each one by smoothing the icing from the outside towards the centre with the bone tool. Set the flowers aside to dry (**a**).

tip You can spread the work of making the flowers, sticking them to the cake and piping the centres over several days if you wish. Remember to wrap your piping bag in clingfilm when you've finished using it to keep it soft for when you need it again.

four Fill a piping bag with some white royal icing and the no.1.5 nozzle (see page 28). Pipe a small dot of royal icing onto the back of each flower so you can stick it to the cake. Starting in the middle of the top tier and working down, place the flowers very close together to cover the whole tier (**b**).

five Stick the flowers to the bottom tier with royal icing as before, leaving a gap of 3–5cm (1–2in) between each one. Add a few flowers to the cakeboard as well (**c**).

six Using the same icing nozzle, pipe a small sugar pearl in the centre of each flower, stopping every few flowers to dab down any icing peaks with a wet paintbrush (**d**).

Simply Inspired...

Simple white sugar flowers make the perfect decoration for cupcakes. You can either ice your cupcakes in vanilla buttercream and create a similar look to the main cake, or choose a contrasting shade of buttercream, such as chocolate, to make the flowers stand out.

tip Sugar flowers will last indefinitely stored in an airtight container. Lay the sugar flowers in the bottom of the container then a layer of kitchen paper, then another layer of flowers, then kitchen paper... until the box is full.

Iced delights

Make your cupcakes and ice with buttercream as explained on page 31. Cut and form your sugar flowers as explained in steps two and three. Allow five or six flowers for each cupcake, leave to dry, then push them gently into the buttercream. Pipe a sugar pearl in the centre of each one with royal icing and the 1.5 nozzle.

Birthday Parcel

I presented this beautiful parcel cake to a friend on her birthday. Knowing how much she loves cake, I was sure it would be a success. Try this deceptively simple and fabulously flamboyant cake on your friends and watch them come flocking (or why not give yourself a pressie!). The beauty of this design is that it can be made in any shape or size. Simply wrap an icing bow around it and, 'ta-da', you have an instant gift!

Materials

One, 20cm (8in) square white iced cake, set onto a 25cm (10in) iced and ribboned cake board (see pages 14–23)

White flowerpaste, 300g (10½oz)

White sugarpaste, 200g (7oz)

Royal icing (see page 28)

Cream food colouring

Equipment

No.1.5 icing nozzle

Scriber needle

Pins

Stay fresh plastic mat

Small paintbrush

a

one Mix the flowerpaste and sugarpaste together well. Add cream food colouring until it turns a soft ivory colour, adding only a tiny amount at a time. Roll out the icing in a long thin shape about 1–2mm (¹/₁₆in) thick.

two Cut a 7.5 x 24cm (3 x 9½in) strip and dust with snowflake lustre. Remove the trimmings and wrap up in cling film to prevent them drying out (**a**).

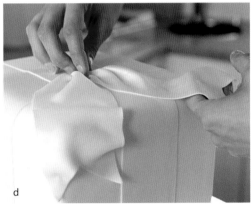

three Find the centre of one side of the cake and make a small pin prick at the base. Using the paintbrush, cover the un-lustred side of the icing strip with water. Apply to the side of the cake using the pin prick as a marker for the centre. Gently ease the end of the icing strip underneath the cake with a small knife to give the impression the ribbon is tied around the cake, and smooth the other end down on the top (**b**).

four Cut three more strips the same size and apply them to the other sides of the cake in the same way. Smooth the ends down carefully over each other on the top of the cake in a neat and centred finish (**c**).

five To make the bow, roll out two, 7.5 x 22.5cm (3 x 9in) strips, two, 7.5 x 20cm (3 x 8in) strips and one, 7.5 x 4cm (3 x 1½in) strip from the trimmings set aside earlier. Lustre all the strips and set under a plastic mat to prevent them drying out.

six Cut an upside down V shape in the end of each 7.5 x 22.5cm (3 x 9in) strip to make a tassel end. Pinch the other ends together, dab water on the back using the paintbrush, and arrange them in the centre of the cake with the tassel ends tumbling over the corners of the cake and slightly gathered as shown (**d**).

seven Take the two, 7.5 x 20cm (3 x 8in) strips, fold each one in half and pinch the ends. Put them together to make a bow and wrap the smallest icing strip around the middle. Add a little more water to the centre of the cake and arrange the bow on top, using pieces of tissue paper to hold the icing in position while it dries (**e**).

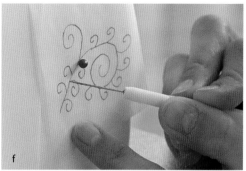

f

g

eight To decorate the sides of the cake, trace the paisley template on page 134 onto a small square of greaseproof paper. Fix the paper to the cake with a pin and score the image onto the cake using the scriber needle or a pin (**f**).

nine Fill a piping bag with royal icing and the no.1.5 nozzle (see page 28). Pipe the design onto the cake following the marked pattern. Dab down any icing peaks with a little water (**g**).

This delightful bow is a gorgeous finishing touch and will make this cake the perfect gift for any occasion.

Simply Inspired...

tip To make coloured bows, add small amounts of food colouring to the mixed white pastes.

These simple cupcakes decorated with pretty icing ribbons look gorgeous grouped together, and are a fabulous variation on the more formal parcel cake. They will make wonderful gifts or party bag treats presented in individual cellophane wraps tied with satin ribbon.

Cupcake Bows

I chose chocolate flavour cupcakes to go with my ivory bows because I think ivory and chocolate brown is a gorgeous colour combination. Make your cupcakes and decorate them with chocolate buttercream as explained on page 31. Make each bow using four, 2.5 x 7cm (1 x 2¾in) icing strips and one smaller strip, as explained in steps five to seven on the previous page. Add them to your cupcakes with a little water.

Simply satin

If you don't have time to make a sugar bow for your cake, place a beautiful satin ribbon around it and tie in a bow. Instead of piping patterns over the cake, look out for pretty embellishments that can be removed just before the cake is cut, like this delicate butterfly. For more inspiration, see page 130.

Brights

Wedding Sunflowers

For me, sunflowers are one of the most joyful flowers in nature, and I couldn't think of a better flower for decorating a wedding cake. I wanted to combine the feel of relaxing, halcyon, summer days with a more traditional design. The flowers are made with a sunflower cutter and have piped icing centres. They are attached to the cake with royal icing and have piped leaves and stalks. The result is a stunning design for a magical occasion.

Materials

One, 15cm (6in), one 20cm (8in) and one, 25cm (10in) double depth round white iced cake, stacked and set onto a 38cm (15in) iced and ribboned board (see pages 14–29)

White flowerpaste, 450g (1lb)

Royal icing (see page 28)

Spruce green, melon yellow, egg yellow and dark brown food colouring

10mm (½in) white satin ribbon

Equipment

Sunflower plunger cutter, 70mm (2¾in)

No.4 and No.43 icing nozzles

Scriber needle or a pin

Bone tool

Flower foam pad

Green florists tape

Thick gage green wire

Thin gage green wire

Small paintbrush

a

one Mix egg yellow and melon yellow food colouring with the white flowerpaste to make sunflower yellow. Start with a small amount of colouring and work more in to create the shade you need. Roll the icing out about 1mm (¹/₁₆in) thick on a plastic board dusted with icing sugar.

two Cut two flowers to make each sunflower using the cutter. For this three-tiered cake you will need 24 sunflowers, plus one more for the top of the cake. Place each one on the foam pad and indent the petals using the attached plunger (**a**).

three Smooth the end of each petal toward the centre of the flower on the foam pad with the bone tool. Place a flower on a dusted plastic tray, dab a little water in the centre and place a second flower on top so that the petals below remain visible. Repeat with all the sunflowers, but on one of them, place some thick florists wire between the two layers of petals. This will be the flower for the top tier. Set all the flowers aside to dry (**b**).

four Mix up some royal icing with dark brown food colouring. Fill a piping bag with the no.43 nozzle and the brown icing (see page 28). Pipe the centre of each flower with little peaked dots (**c**).

five Mix a small amount of flowerpaste with some spruce green food colouring (add a tiny amount of melon yellow for a slightly brighter green). Trace the leaf template on page 134. Roll out the icing and cut out two leaves for the top sunflower using the template and a sharp knife. On the foam pad, curl the edges of the leaves with the bone tool.

tip Make a couple of extra flowers and leaves in case you have any breakages.

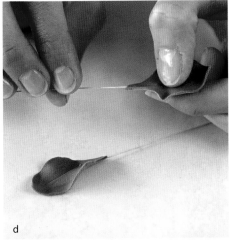

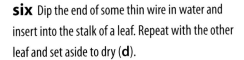

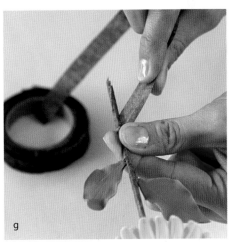

six Dip the end of some thin wire in water and insert into the stalk of a leaf. Repeat with the other leaf and set aside to dry (**d**).

seven Plan where your sunflowers will go before you stick any on the cake. Space them evenly around each tier. Put some royal icing in a piping bag (no nozzle needed), and stick the first sunflower to the side of the top tier. Using your scriber tool (or pin), score the outline of the stem and two leaves onto the cake just below (**e**).

eight Mix some royal icing with some spruce green and melon yellow food colouring, to make the same colour as the leaves. Fill a piping bag with the icing and the no.4 nozzle.

nine Pipe along the scored lines on the cake. Pipe the outline of the leaf and fill the centre. Use a little water to dab the icing down and remove any visible piped lines (**f**).

ten Add all the sunflowers to your cake in this way. Gently wind green florists tape around the stem of the wired sunflower for the top tier. Work downwards, adding the wired leaves on the way. Carefully push this into the cake. To prevent the icing cracking, use a skewer to make a small hole first (**g**).

Simply Inspired...

You can create a lighter, more informal design that's perfect for a girls' tea party by using a single tier cake and icing it in a different colour. I chose a simple daisy for this design, but you could use other flowers. Choose a flat flower (for example, a daisy, gerbera, or sunflower) that will sit easily on the side of the cake.

Sunny cupcakes

These sugar sunflowers lend themselves perfectly to cupcakes. I chose vanilla buttercream icing to complement the bright yellow flowers. Make your sunflowers following steps one to four as before and leave to dry. Bake your cupcakes and spread with buttercream icing (see page 31). Carefully place a flower on top of each cupcake and put out for everyone to enjoy.

Daisy, daisy

The flower heads on the daisy cake, opposite, are made in the same way as the sunflowers, only with a single layer of petals. I used ruby food colouring to create my dark pink flowers and mixed the flowerpaste with a little sugarpaste. Cut out the flowers and form the petals with the bone tool as explained in step three, then set aside to dry. Follow steps seven to nine to decorate your cake. Pipe the centre of each flower with royal icing mixed with a tiny amount of ruby colouring using a piping bag with a no.3 nozzle.

tip Experiment with different colour combinations for your icing flowers to find what works well together, or suits your party or event. Orange flowers with bright pink centres make a dramatic contrast, for example.

Retro Circles

Here is another colour scheme for the boys. I love the combination of blue, brown and cream, and the contrast between the square cake and the circles works really well, too. This is one of my husband's favourite cake designs and, as you can imagine, he's seen a lot of cakes!

Materials

One 20cm (8in) square blue iced cake (or size of your choice), set onto a blue iced cake board 7.5cm (3in) larger than the cake (see pages 14–29)

White sugarpaste, 150g (5oz)

Dark brown food colouring

Cream food colouring

Brown satin ribbon

Equipment

Circle cutters, five different sizes

No.3 icing nozzle

Small paintbrush

a

one Mix up some blue icing leftover from covering the cake and cake board (see pages 20–24) with some water to make a paste with a royal icing consistency. Place in a piping bag with a no.3 nozzle (see page 28). Snail trail around the edge of the cake as explained on page 29.

two Divide the sugarpaste into two balls and mix one with a tiny amount of cream food colouring and the other with enough dark brown food colouring to make a chocolate colour. Roll each one out about 2mm ($^{1}/_{16}$in) thick (**a**).

b

c

tip You can buy sugarpaste icing in a range of colours like the blue used here from sugarcraft suppliers and well stocked supermarkets. You can also colour your own icing if you prefer.

three Use the circle cutters to cut out a series of different size cream and brown circles. Cut out the centre of the larger circles with the next smallest cutter and leave the small circles as solid dots (**b**).

four Now plan the design of your cake. You can create an interesting pattern by spacing the circles randomly, interlocking two together and cutting the solid dots in half. Wet the back of each circle before sticking it onto the cake. Avoid adding too much water in case it seeps out the sides and leaves a mark (**c**).

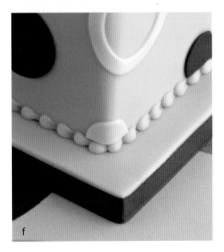

tip Decide where you want the circles to go before sticking them on. Once you have stuck a circle onto the cake, you won't be able to remove it without leaving a water mark behind, especially with the chocolate ones.

five To interlock two circles, lay a circle on a board dusted with icing sugar and hold another one over it. Cut two gaps in the circle underneath and slot the top one into it. Wet the back and carefully stick them to the cake (**d**).

six Stick some of the circles so they overlap the sides and corners of the cake as well. Wet the back as before and gently smooth the circle down on each side of the cake in turn. Try to keep the round shape of the circle because they can go a little egg-shaped (**e**).

seven Cut a few solid circles in half with a sharp knife and stick these with a little water to the sides of the cake, lining up the straight edge with the snail trail. Measure the circumference of your cake board and stick brown ribbon around it as explained on page 29 (**f**).

For the girls

Retro circles work equally well on a square or round cake.
White ribbon was just right to complete this brightly coloured
round version of the design.

Simply Inspired...

For an alternative effect, try cutting your retro circles and dots from raspberry and tangerine icing. They contrast beautifully with a white iced cake. You can also make mini cakes instead of a large cake and decorate them with circles and dots.

Mini retro

Mini cakes make an easy and fun alternative to the main design. See page 32 for advice on making mini cakes and the recipes on pages 14–17. Cut a series of icing circles and dots the right size for your mini cakes, and stick them in place as explained in steps two to six. Finish off each cake with a narrow brown ribbon (see page 29).

Rouge

Bright colours on a white cake make for a very dramatic effect. Fun red flowers and firework swirls form a great partnership with pink and red ribbon. Dress your cake with matching fresh flowers and think about adding a few indoor sparklers to the display, then watch the whole cake sparkle and swirl. The perfect party cake!

one Measure round each tier and cut some red ribbon this size plus a little extra. Wrap it around the base and secure with royal icing (see page 29). Add pink ribbon on top to form a stripe. Repeat on the cakeboard.

two Mix the flowerpaste and sugarpaste together. Add enough red food colouring to turn it a deep red. Roll out the icing 1–2mm (1/16in) thick and keep it moist under a stay fresh mat.

three Make about 12 flowers with each size cutter. Stick them onto the cake with a little water. Allow enough space between the flowers for the swirls (**a**).

Materials

One, 15cm (6in) and one, 25cm (10in) round white iced cake, stacked and set onto a 35.5cm (14in) iced cake board (see pages 14–25)
Sugarpaste, 50g (1¾oz)
Flowerpaste, 50g (1¾oz)
Royal icing (see page 28)
Red food colouring
10mm (½in) red ribbon
5mm (¼in) pink ribbon
Fresh flowers

Equipment

Flower cutters, three sizes
No.1.5 icing nozzle
Scriber needle
Small rolling pin
Stay fresh plastic mat
Small paintbrush
Florists wire

tip If you want to make some cupcakes to match, mix a little more icing and set aside for later.

b

c

four Add red food colouring to the royal icing to make the same shade of red as the flowers. Prepare a piping bag with the 1.5 nozzle (see page 28) and pipe the centres of the flowers with small dots. Using a little water, dab down the icing peaks with a wet paintbrush (**b**).

five Trace the swirl template on page 134 onto greaseproof paper, pin this to the cake where you want the first swirl to go, and score the image with a scriber needle or a pin. Remove the paper and repeat around the cake (**c**).

d

six Pipe tiny dots of red royal icing along each scored swirl. Dab down the icing peaks as you go along (**d**).

tip When attaching the flowers to your cake, check your paintbrush isn't dripping wet because the water may bleed out of the flower afterwards and leave a mark.

tip Choose flowers to match the colour scheme of your cake. Here I used fresh roses and Gloriosa lily, but silk flowers will work equally well.

seven Cut off the heads of the flowers for the top of the cake, and gently push them into a small ball of icing stuck to the top of the cake. You can also use florists wire to insert them into the cake if you prefer (**e**).

Flowers look wonderful on top of a cake, especially roses, which add height and volume to the design.

Simply Inspired...

tip If you don't have time to score and pipe swirls on your cake, add some individual sugar pearls instead when you're piping the flower centres.

Using a different colour scheme completely alters the character or mood of a cake design. Here, contrasting shades of soft mint green and deep chocolate brown give a light and airy, modern feel to this cake. And cupcakes topped with buttercream and bright red flowers will make a real impact on a party table!

Minty fresh

The flowers on this single tier version of the design were cut from icing coloured with a hint of mint green as explained in steps two to four.

Red sensation

Friends will love to take one of your cupcakes to enjoy at home later. It will only take a minute to pack some up in clear boxes and tie with an organza ribbon. Make your cupcakes and ice with vanilla buttercream (see page 31). Roll out the remaining red icing and cut out one large and one small flower per cake. Pipe the flower centres and a few extra dots for decoration.

Candy Stripes

This cake design reminds me of a beautiful box filled with chocolates a gentleman might give to his sweetheart. And the sugar roses look like a corsage for a High School Prom. The design will work with any colour scheme – naturally, I have chosen my favourite! The cake is simple to decorate; it is the sugar flowers that you will need to devote a little time to. If you are in a hurry, perhaps use some fresh flowers or pipe a birthday message on top of the cake.

a

one Place the smaller cake board over the cake. Check it is centred then score round it using a scriber needle or pin (**a**).

tip If you don't have the right size cake board to score round, use a plate or saucer instead. It doesn't have to be exactly 5cm (2in) smaller than the cake.

Materials

One, round white iced cake set onto a white iced and ribboned cake board, 7.5cm (3in) larger than the cake (see pages 14–29)

Thin cake board, 5cm (2in) smaller than the cake

Sugarpaste, 300g (10½oz)

Flowerpaste, 150g (5oz)

Royal icing (see page 28)

Pink and melon yellow food colouring

Flower stamens

Equipment

Rose petal cutters, two sizes

No.1.5 icing nozzle

Small paintbrush

Flower foam pad

Bone tool

Stay fresh plastic mat

Small rolling pin

Ruler

Scriber needle

Small sharp knife

Small polystyrene pieces

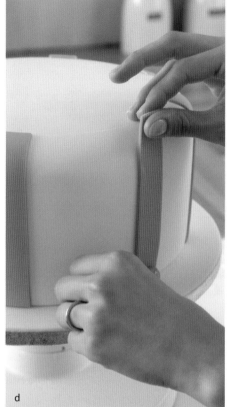

two Mix some pink food colouring with the sugarpaste until it is deep candy pink. Roll out until it is about 2mm (¹/₁₆in) thick and keep moist under a stay fresh mat. Measure the height of the cake from the board to the scored line. Using a ruler, or an oblong cutter, cut out 16, 2.5cm (1in) strips this length (**b**).

three Brush the back of each strip with a little water and stick it to the side of the cake. Stick on two opposite strips at the same time to help you space them evenly (**c**).

four Put some white royal icing in a piping bag with a no.1.5 nozzle. Using the scored line and the top of the stripes as a guide, pipe a small snail trail around the top of the cake (see page 28) (**d**).

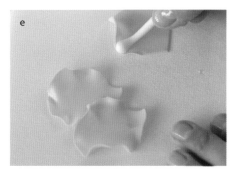

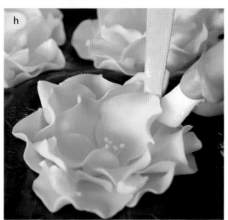

five Mix yellow food colouring with the flowerpaste to make the sugar flowers. Roll it out about 2mm (1/16in) thick and cut out nine rose petals, five large and four smaller ones, to make the first rose. Put the petals on the foam pad and feather the edges with the bone tool (**e**).

six Wet the backs of the petals and arrange them on top of each other in a rose shape. A supermarket apple tray makes an ideal base for this. Make two more roses the same way (**f**).

seven Cut six stamens about 1.5cm (½in) long and stick in the centre of one rose. Repeat on the other two flowers (**g**).

eight Place several small pieces of polystyrene or rolled up kitchen paper between the petals to keep them in position while they harden. Leave overnight (**h**).

nine Gently remove the polystyrene and stick the flowers on top of the cake with some royal icing (**i**).

Simply Inspired...

Candy stripes go well on cakes for many different occasions. Here, primrose yellow stripes make the perfect accompaniment for a delicious Easter cake topped with a chocolate nest filled with mini eggs.

Materials

200g (7oz) milk chocolate

25g (1oz) dark chocolate

25g (1oz) butter

125g (4½oz) shredded wheat

Easter nests

Make your cupcakes and cover with buttercream as explained on page 31. Decorate your cake with candy stripes as explained in steps one to four, using melon yellow food colouring instead of pink, and tie on some raffia. Place the chocolate and butter in a bowl and melt over boiling water. Crush the shredded wheat and mix into the chocolate. Leave to cool slightly. Lay a sheet of greaseproof paper on a tray, place a handful of the chocolate mix onto it and form round nest shapes to fit the top of your cake and cupcakes. Pop in some chocolate mini eggs to create the perfect Easter nest. Set aside to cool and set, out of the fridge. Place the nests on top of your cakes.

Children adore my Easter cupcakes decorated with chocolate nests.

tip The size of your cake will determine how many candy stripes you need, so measure the circumference before you start cutting the strips. They should be spaced evenly around the cake.

Cupcake Treats

Cupcakes are so versatile. You can dress them up or down to suit any occasion. Smooth icing and a perfect sugar rose work well for a formal tea party or wedding, but for a scrumptious treat, cover them in indulgent buttercream or chocolate ganache! I've given some ideas on how to decorate cupcakes throughout the book, but here is a whole cupcake tower that's just the thing for any party or gathering.

Materials
Cupcakes covered with buttercream (see pages 14–18 and 31)
Flowerpaste
Sugarpaste
Pink and spruce green food colouring
Lustre, pink or snowflake
Edible glitter

Equipment
Star cutters
Heart cutters
Small rolling pin
Small paintbrush

one Make your cupcakes and cover each one with buttercream as explained on page 31 (**a**).

two To make the hearts and stars, mix some flowerpaste with pink food colouring. Roll it out 3mm (¹/₈in) thick and cut out your stars, brush the top of each one with a wet paintbrush, dip it into a plate of pink glitter and set aside to dry (**b**).

three Cut out your hearts from the same icing and dust each one with lustre (either pink or snowflake) using a paintbrush.

tip When colouring icing, avoid streaks by first mixing a small amount of white icing with a large amount of food colouring; mix this concentrated colour with more white icing.

125

four To make the roses, mix equal amounts of flowerpaste and sugarpaste and add pink colouring to make the same shade as before. Shape small balls of the pink icing and flatten them out with your fingers to make petals, keeping the edges neat. Curl the first petal around to form the centre bud of your rose, then wrap further petals around it. See also page 82, steps 7 and 8.

five Brush the tips of the sugar rose petals with water and dip into a dish of pink glitter. Mix a little spruce green food colouring with some flowerpaste and roll out about 2mm ($^1/_{16}$in) thick. Cut out a star shape to make a calyx for each rose. Place the roses in the centre of the stars and stick with a little water (**c**).

six Gently push your decorations into the buttercream on your cupcakes.

Brush the tips of the sugar rose petals with water and dip into a dish of pink glitter. If you would prefer, you can use different colour glitter to complement your colour scheme.

You can use any shape or size cutter for cupcakes. And if you stick to the same colour icing for all the decorations it makes a truly gorgeous display.

Simply Inspired...

You can vary a favourite cake design to suit a particular occasion simply by choosing different colours for the icing. It's so easy to make cupcakes decorated with stars or roses for any mood or season.

Sunny yellow

These sunny yellow roses are perfect for every celebration, from a wedding to Easter and Mother's Day. You can dress them up for a formal occasion with gold muffin cases and a matching ribbon.

Ice blue

For the coolest birthday cakes in town, mix some baby blue food colouring with sugarpaste and use to cut out stars to go on the top of your cupcakes. This simple idea will look even more effective if you add a small indoor sparkler as well.

Spring green

These cupcakes decorated with sugar stars in a lovely fresh shade of green are just right for an early summer picnic. The stars are made from sugarpaste mixed with mint green food colouring and dipped in matching glitter.

Deep purple

For a magical effect at a Bonfire Night or Christmas party, try making cupcakes decorated with glistening wine-coloured roses. I used grape violet food colouring to create a rich shade of purple and formed my flowers as explained in steps four and five on page 126.

Ready to Wear...

There's no reason why you must only use sugar decorations on your cakes. I have a large box containing satin and velvet ribbons, silk flowers, jewels, feather butterflies and birds, and many other wonderful pieces I have collected over time which I love to dip into for inspiration for my designs. I view a plain iced cake as a blank canvas to do whatever I choose with. You can buy any of the items I've used here at most well stocked haberdashers or craft stores. See Suppliers on page 135 for details.

Silk flowers

You can now buy silk flowers that are so beautiful it doesn't feel like a compromise to use them. Adding one or two large silk flowers to a cake creates a dramatic effect, especially if you choose a shade you wouldn't normally associate with fresh flowers, such as black or aqua marine blue. They are also very practical because they won't wilt and can be used again.

Diamante crystals

I love to use jewels in my designs: they are a perfect way to add a little extra sparkle and Hollywood glamour to a cake. Always make sure that any diamantes or jewels are removed before the cake is served.

tip Bought, non-edible decorations are quick and easy to use but have a lasting impact. After the cake has been eaten, they will make perfect mementos of the day.

This chic centerpiece is created with icing candy stripes (see page 120) and silk roses, all in the same soft shade of ivory as the cake. Wrapping diamantes around the base of each tier instead of ribbon adds the final touch of glamour.

More Ready to Wear...

Embellished ribbon

Dressing a simple ivory cake with a wide satin sash and bow creates a design that is understated yet very stylish. You can use ribbon to tie in your cake with a particular colour scheme. If it is for a wedding, for example, match your ribbon to a sash around a bridesmaid's dress or the colour of a rose in the bride's bouquet.

Layering ribbon

You can buy many different types of ribbon, from plain to embellished styles, which are perfect for wrapping around a cake. For a special finishing touch, try layering a narrow embellished ribbon over a wider one.

Butterflies

Sparkling butterflies are available in a range of different colours. Why not buy some in contrasting shades to decorate a series of cupcakes and display them on a stand.

Bright spark

These mini indoor sparklers can be bought in heart and star shapes and make a change from traditional candles.

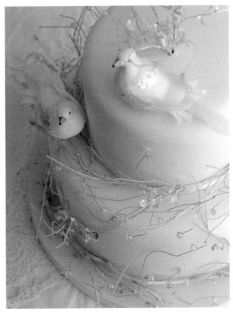

Jewels

Make a wedding or birthday cake look extra special by decorating it with a surprise gift of a jewelled ribbon bow.

Love birds

Feather birds and butterflies are useful for incorporating the chosen theme for a party or wedding in a cake design.

Templates

Here are the templates you will need for some of the designs in the book.
Transfer them onto the cake with a scriber needle or pin ready for piping.

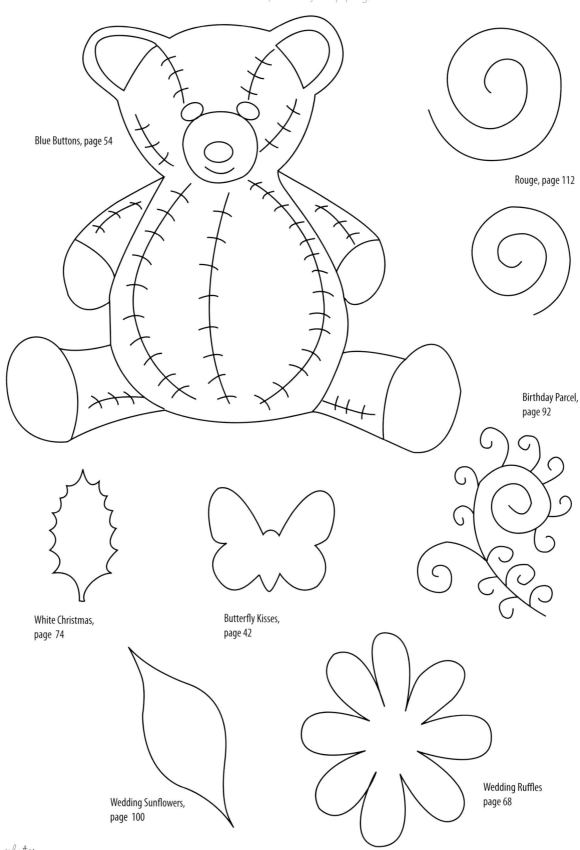

Blue Buttons, page 54

Rouge, page 112

Birthday Parcel,
page 92

White Christmas,
page 74

Butterfly Kisses,
page 42

Wedding Sunflowers,
page 100

Wedding Ruffles
page 68

Suppliers

UK

Maisie Fantaisie
Tel: 020 8671 5858
www.maisiefantaisie.co.uk

For general sugarcraft materials:

Knightsbridge PME Ltd
Chadwell Heath Lane
Romford
Essex
RN6 4NP
Tel: 020 8590 5959
www.cakedecoration.co.uk

Squires Kitchen
Squires House
3 Waverley Lane
Farnham
Surrey
GU9 8BB
Tel: 0845 22 55 671
www.squires-group.co.uk

Surbiton Art and Sugarcraft
140 Hook Road
Surbiton
Surrey
KT6 5BZ
Tel: 020 8391 4664
www.surbitonart.co.uk

For ribbons and feathers

John Lewis
Haberdashery Department
www.johnlewis.com for nearest
store finder

VV Rouleax
54 Sloane Square
London
SW1W 8AX
Tel: 020 7730 3125
www.vvrouleaux.com

For Floristry:

Mathew Dickinson
Cabin J
25 Horsell Road
London
N5 1XJ
Tel: 020 7503 0456
www.mathewdickinsonflowers.com

US

Pfeil and Holing
58–15 Northern Boulevard
Woodside
NY 11377
Tel: (718) 545-4600/ (800) 247-7955
www.cakedeco.com

New York Cake Supplies
56 West 22nd Street
New York
NY 10010
Tel: (800) 942-2539/ (212) 675-2253
www.nycake.com

Sweet Celebrations
PO Box 39426
Edina
MN 55436,
Tel: (800) 328-6722
www.sweetc.com

Acknowledgments

It's simply a pleasure for me to have to think about all of the lovely people who have helped me get this far with my cake decorating business and my first cake decorating book.

Firstly I would like to give huge thanks to my parents for always allowing me to make my own decisions and supporting me with every choice I've made. My Sister who has been, and still is, a huge inspiration to me in every way possible.

When I first started making cakes, I was lucky enough to work with a very talented cake maker, Kate Poulter. Thank you Kate, without you none of this would have been possible.

Kate Smallwood I would like to give thanks to for watering a fledging Maisie Fantaisie and watching it bloom. The same thanks goes to Mathew Dickinson for his guidance and support in those early show days.

I would like to say a big thank you to Jenny, Sarah and Beth at David & Charles for asking me to collaborate with them and create what is now a beautiful book to be proud of. Thank you, also, to Ginette Chapman, my photographer for taking the most perfect shots of my cakes.

And more recently I would like to thank Jenny Barr for bringing so much to Maisie Fantaisie.

Big thumbs up to Felix and Mia for being sweeter than my cakes.

And lastly, but certainly not least, the biggest thanks to my husband Daron for all his positivity. His help and support has made Maisie Fantaisie the wonderful cake world it is today.

About the Author

May Clee-Cadman founded Maisie Fantaisie in 2003 to create unique wedding and celebration cakes. She studied Art and Design History graduating with an honours degree in 2000, and went on to train as a cake designer incorporating her flair for design with her love of cake making.

Index